A Journey of Hats

Devotionals for Single Women
Who've Been Touched by Breast Cancer

WRITTEN BY

Loretta J. Barr

A Journey of Hats
Loretta J. Barr

Copyright © 2020 by Loretta J. Barr, All rights reserved.

No part of this book may be reproduced by photocopy or any other means without the written permission of Loretta J. Barr.

Scripture quotations marked (NIV) are taken from the Holy Bible, New International Version®, NIV®. Copyright © 1973, 1978, 1984, 2011 by Biblica, Inc.™ Used by permission of Zondervan. All rights reserved worldwide. www.zondervan.com The "NIV" and "New International Version" are trademarks registered in the United States Patent and Trademark Office by Biblica, Inc.™

Scripture taken from the New King James Version®. Copyright © 1982 by Thomas Nelson. Used by permission. All rights reserved.

ISBN: 978-1-7341862-1-5

CONTENTS

Dedication v
Introduction 1
   How to Use These Devotionals 3
   What if You're not a Believer? 4

Beginning the Journey

What You've Feared Most 7
   Message to Caregivers: 9
The Lone Warrior 11
   Message to Caregivers, Family and Friends: 13
Is There a Blessing in Breast Cancer? 15

When You Begin Your Treatment

God's Battle 19
Joy in the Midst of the Storm 23
   Message to Caregivers: 24
Unwanted Membership 27
What about the Side Effects? 31

LIFE AFTER TREATMENT...

Being Brave in Other Areas of Your Life ... 37
    Dating ... 37
    Job Loss ... 38
Your Daily Realities ... 41
Fighting Cancer a Second Time ... 45
God's Faithfulness ... 49

ANSWERING YOUR CALLING

Journey to Recovery ... 53

DEDICATION

To my church for recognizing that ministry comes in many forms—especially in the guise of writers and the writers' community in all its iterations.

To Earma for kindling my tiny creative spark and Tracey for igniting the spark into a flame through both word and action. To Felecia for her steadfast example of calmness and resilience. To Yvonne, my persistent friend, who walked with me both times on my cancer journey. To Leslie for her steadfast support during my second journey. And, to Carole and Kim who would not let me give up my desire to write. All have taught me the importance of staying true to one's craft and God's calling.

To my sisters in Christ in Write Direction and Write Now, Connie, Latarsha, and Alveta for your inspiration, support and help in crafting my message.

To my parents, Catherine and Jimmie whose work ethic preserved me and witness encouraged me. To my family, through all its iterations, ups and downs, and many challenges. To my sister, Jennie—a model of God's provision and His grace—you are centered in my prayers.

And, finally—but most importantly—to the Holy Spirit for His call, guidance and comfort.

INTRODUCTION

Going through breast cancer is a frightening experience with many twists and turns unique to each survivor's circumstances. And, every survivor has different coping mechanisms for enduring the day-to-day trials and the side effects. Hats happen to be mine. Hats represent physical protection for the head and metaphorically protection for the mind. What else do hats represent to me?

- **Keeping me in my right mind** as I prepared daily for the next steps.
- **Keeping my humor intact** as I recognized laughter as an integral part of my life.
- **Reminding me of my fight** by being part of my protective gear.

Hats became my go-to emblem during my own two fights with breast cancer. During my first journey with cancer and I lost my hair, I tried wearing a wig for all of one day. I went into the office with a crazy looking bob-cut hair piece that itched like everything. By noon I was rubbing my temples. By three o'clock, my wig was sideways. By 6 pm when I left the office, I drove by Target, bought a straw hat and tossed the wig on the passenger's seat. I never wore it again. The following day, my team raved over my hat and later that week, presented me with a gift certificate to buy more. With my second journey with breast cancer, my friends showed up at my home, threw a surprise hat party and brought TEN hats. They then divided up cooking and care duties for the duration of my chemo treatments. God surely provided. My breast cancer journey has been and still is one as a woman with no kids, no spouse, no parents and no siblings nearby. But though I'm single, God is with me and He has used my hats as helmets for my battle. He has provided my help through friends, coworkers and church in amazing ways.

Consider what a simple thing a hat is. Yet it speaks volumes in personality, utility and purpose. And, it doesn't stop there. You may have hats for other uses: working outside, going to the beach or covering a "bad hair day." In the African American churches I attended growing up, magnificent hats adorned the heads of church-going black women. It was tradition and pageantry. It was showing your best to God on His day - colorful and beautifully arrayed like the lilies of the field. Your own troubles, heartbreaks, and pains were set aside as you worshiped God in all His glory. Your hat became your symbolic helmet of salvation during your worship. While it's true there aren't so many hats in church today, putting on your Sunday best in body, spirit and mind still stands. What hat you choose (or not) for your breast cancer journey is up to you.

How to Use These Devotionals

A Journey of Hats Devotionals is designed to offer a place of respite while you are fighting breast cancer. The devotionals I've written are from my own experiences and represent my truth. You will most certainly find your own. When I was first diagnosed, I knew of no one who had personally gone through the disease, so I had an overwhelming feeling of aloneness. I want you to know that these feelings can be overcome through leaning on the Word. Scriptural references as revealed by the Holy Spirit accompany each devotional and there is note space for you to add yours. The goal is for you to stay in the Word and be spiritually grounded throughout your battle. Throughout the devotionals are messages for caregivers should you need to help them help you. As you progress through your journey, there will be days where your personal scriptures will be your anchors.

What if You're Not a Believer?

If you are new on your faith journey or never started one, that's okay. This is the time to lean in and ask for God's help. A good starting point is John 3:16 to know how God loves you and Luke 7:7 to ask and keep asking for God's leading. Romans 10:9-10 will help you take the next steps in receiving God's promise.

Associate your scripture with your hat (or whatever item you choose) and the stage of your journey. Let's begin.

"For I know the plans I have for you," declares the Lord, "plans to prosper you and not to harm you, plans to give you a hope and future."
- Jeremiah 29:11 (NIV)

Beginning the Journey

WHAT YOU'VE FEARED MOST

Breast cancer. Two words that send chills down your spine and paralyze you with fear. You are in shock. Disbelief. You ask yourself over and over "Why?" You are overwhelmed with emotions, fearing the worst and wanting a release from the nightmare. You may not know anyone who has experienced cancer. Or worst, you know of family members who had it. Breast cancer. It's real. It's frightening. It's touched you. What now?

Fear is a natural response when receiving any cancer diagnosis and breast cancer is no exception. Your fear can cripple your decision making and cause you not to tell anyone. Don't. You may also feel alone. You're not. As you face a diagnosis of breast cancer, there are scriptural resting places to consider:

> *"Have I not commanded you? Be strong and of good courage; do not be afraid, nor be dismayed, for the Lord your God is with you wherever you go."*
> **- Joshua 1:9**

"Beloved, I pray that you may prosper in all things and be in health, just as your soul prospers."

- 3 John 1:2

Facing a cancer diagnosis with courage doesn't mean you are without fear. It means that while you are afraid and while you are anxious, you meditate and seek God's counsel. Ask Him to direct your path and guide your decisions.

"Your word is a lamp to my feet and a light to my path."

- Psalm 119:105

"I will say of the Lord, "He is my refuge and my fortress, my God, in whom I trust."

- Psalm 91:2 (NIV)

"I lift up my eyes to the mountains—where does my help come from? My help comes from the Lord, the Maker of heaven and earth."

- Psalm 121:1-2 (NIV)

Message to Caregivers:

If someone you know is facing breast cancer, please know this news is devastating. Be mindful of that fact and acknowledge it. Know also that for believers the news of breast cancer or any disease is not the end. Believers know that we have a Savior who can rid us of this disease or use it to His glory. Help the person in your care know that there is comfort and place of refuge in Jesus. The fear she is experiencing may cause her to question her own faith. Walk with her and remind her of whom she is in Christ. Remember, He is with her. He knows what she feels. He heard the news before she did. Remind her to fight the battle in the way God tells her. Tell her to trust Him to write the rest of her story.

My Scriptures and Prayer Requests

THE LONE WARRIOR

"God sets the lonely in families."
- Psalm 68:6a (NIV)

*"Direct my footsteps according to your word;
let no sin rule over me."*
- Psalm 119:133 (NIV)

It's life affirming to know that so many of those who battle breast cancer face it with dignity and courage. Each situation is unique, yet the common thread I've found is that the vast majority of the articles begin with "my husband supported me…" or "my kids…" or "my wife…" I've learned and gleaned wisdom from those touching stories about other women who battled breast cancer while being surrounded by a loving family. But what if you must face your battle with cancer alone? What if you're a single person who has no parents, children or spouse? Must you face your trial alone? I found myself in that very situation both times I experienced breast cancer.

With so many women contracting breast cancer sometime in their lifetime, singles cannot escape the implications. Nevertheless, I'm convinced that there are many unwritten stories about those who didn't have a traditional support group. While I can't speak to how other singles battle cancer solo, I can recount my own experiences. I recall quite vividly my own diagnosis of cancer both times. I didn't think "Why me?", but rather "why alone?" Yet God was with me each time. He blessed me tremendously with the resources I needed to fight my breast cancer physically, financially, emotionally and spiritually.

Here's what I've found:

- God will send the people you need to walk with you in this journey.
- God will show you your persistent friends – those who stick with you no matter what to laugh with you and cry with you.
- God will give you clarity and wisdom about your treatment options.
- God will always be there to listen to you during times of distress, pain and disappointments.
- God will provide blessings along the way. He may choose you to be the blessing.

Message to Caregivers, Family and Friends:

Breast cancer is a devastating disease whether it's fought with a family or alone. In the midst of the battle, God's call to us is clear. Those of us who are breast cancer survivors, caregivers or friends are to share our experiences with those who have been diagnosed and just beginning their treatment.

We should be sensitive to the life circumstances of those touched by breast cancer. It's not enough to assume they have family. We must offer our help and keep on offering. We should send words of encouragement. We need to listen carefully to that still small voice inside us. Oftentimes, others may not voice everything they feel, need or even what they are going through, but the still small voice utters words that are unspoken to those who will listen to Him. The small voice allows us to hear what is not being said by those who need us most.

My Scriptures and Prayer Requests

Is There a Blessing in Breast Cancer?

"Trust in the Lord with all your heart and lean not on your own understanding; In all your ways acknowledge Him, and He shall direct your paths."
- **Proverbs 3:5-6 (NKJV)**

Let's be clear: Cancer is not a blessing. However, there are lessons and blessings we can glean along the way. Mine were multi-faceted. Facing cancer showed me how awesome God was in bringing me through it. I had the blessing of seeing God show Himself through the names we call Him. Here are just a few of the ones that I've witnessed during both seasons:

- Jehovah Jireh: God provides. He provided insurance, awesome colleagues, support, persistence and strength by His grace.
- Jehovah Nissi: God is our banner. He fought my battle and He told me the first time I experienced cancer that the battle was not mine but God's. I believed that truth for my second battle.
- El Shaddai: God Almighty. He has power to overcome anything we experience.

- Elohim: God is our God from the beginning to the end.

The blessings I have are plentiful, but the most important one is life through Christ. It is because of him that I can face each day. The mastectomy, the side effects during and after chemo and the struggles for normalcy are in His hands. I take his hand, put on my hat and live. What about you?

What blessings has God provided to you?

When You Begin Your *Treatment*

God's Battle

"Do not be anxious about anything, but in every situation, by prayer and petition, with thanksgiving, present your requests to God."
- Philippians 4:6 (NIV)

The first thing I saw after coming from under anesthesia was a tangle of tubes `attached to me. Why were there so many? Tubes seemed to protrude from everywhere. My eyes followed the IV tube in my left hand to the medication dispenser, which automatically delivered a concoction of drugs while whirring gently. After the nurses showed me how to operate it, I nicknamed the device Dial-a-Drug. If I felt pain, I could click on a button and no more pain. Of course, it didn't quite work that way.

I watched the nurses come in and out during the night adjusting the Dial-a-Drug and checking my vitals. I was vaguely aware of a compression device that squeezed my toe it seemed every time I dozed. My eyes wandered over to another tube protruding from my right side draining fluids that my missing lymph nodes no longer could. All were casualties from my fight with breast cancer.

Because of suspicious fibroid tumors, I also had gotten a hysterectomy that included exploratory surgery straight up my abdomen to see if those were cancerous. I was sutured with surgical staples. Any movement of my upper torso arrested my attention with pain. I never knew that so many parts of the body used the stomach muscles. It seemed these muscles hurt when I wiggled my toes and batted my eyelids, so I dared not laugh though something about all the tubes did seem a bit humorous. I was a mess.

Yet I marveled at God's amazing timing. I had gone to my doctor for a routine checkup that I almost cancelled. I had not seen a doctor during the seven years of my being self-employed and without health insurance. I knew I had some health issues and expected the fibroid tumors were due for removal. However, a challenge emerged that was completely unexpected – breast cancer. The blur of testing, diagnosing, poking and prodding had culminated in this operation. There I lay, recovering from a hysterectomy, lumpectomy and lymph node surgery. One time under anesthesia with one operation on three different parts of my body – split open like a ripe melon. Scarred by the battle, but still living. Tested by the circumstances, but not forgotten. Filled with tubes, but also filled with God's grace. I found myself clinging to the scripture God gave me a month before I was diagnosed: "For the battle is not yours, but God's." 2Chronicles 20:15 NIV

These steps of my first journey with breast cancer were not easy, but God fought the battle and carried me through. I earned my first hat.

What scripture(s) has God laid on your heart?

My Scriptures and Prayer Requests

Joy in the Midst of the Storm

"And He said to me, 'My grace is sufficient for you, for My strength is made perfect in weakness. 'Therefore most gladly I will rather boast in my infirmities, that the power of Christ may rest upon me."
- 2 Corinthians 12:9 (NKJV)

Through the pain, the countless tests and the maze of treatments, God is still with you as He has been with me. As you move through your treatment, you may feel as if you are moving from a storm to a tsunami, but God still has you. I've witnessed His grace comfort those who fought multiple battles with breast cancer, and I've come to realize some amazing truths you can count on:

God is still in control. You can be certain He knows the outcome. Place your trust in Him to guide you through your journey

God wastes no suffering. The incredible, brave warriors who encouraged me during both my cancer fights are the reason I'm able to encourage others. He will be the reason you can encourage others.

God never leaves us. He is with us even when there is no miraculous cure. He is with us even when our loved ones go away to be with Him. Faith is trust not denial. God may not heal every disease, but

He can heal every broken heart, He may not answer a prayer the way we expect, but He can comfort every downtrodden spirit. He may not remove the disappointments, but He can soothe every hurting soul. Faith is believing God's promises in spite of the circumstances or the outcomes.

Message to Caregivers:

For those who are walking with family or friends facing cancer, be an encourager with care and sensitivity. Rather than sharing how cancer has taken your own loved ones, support those who are still in the fight. We serve a God of hope. Move from some simply surviving your cancer to thriving as a warrior knowing God is there. He is in the battle with you.

Who is fighting this fight with you?

My Scriptures and Prayer Requests

Unwanted Membership

*"Search me, God, and know my heart; test me
and know my anxious thoughts."*
- Psalm 139:23 (NIV)

In 1977, I pledged Delta Sigma Theta sorority when I was still in college. I remember the exhilaration of making the commitment, of being selected and of crossing the "burning sand." I chose to join that sorority and they chose to induct me. We were sisters for life. I saw other male friends of mine endure a similar induction process into their fraternities, walking in lines, wearing pledgee T-shirts, carrying pledge paraphernalia and competing in Greek shows as we did. These activities were deliberate choices with deliberate and desired outcomes. Bonds were developed among these groups that would last a lifetime.

In 1999, I joined another sorority. This sorority had members who did not choose to join and did not choose to be inducted. Yet in that year alone over 213,000 women and 1,450 men joined the sorority and fraternity of those diagnosed with breast cancer. And if those statistics were not enough, an estimated 40,970 women and 460 men will die from the disease. While there may be bonds developed that last a lifetime among those who have contracted this disease, the real aim is overcoming and surviving.

Breast cancer will attack one in seven women over their lifetimes.[1] Many will win the battle; some won't. Still, for those of us who follow Christ, we have His promises:

Healing if God chooses to. Comfort always. Someone to share the load through Jesus and He will set the lonely in families. This is true even for those who fight the battle with family members standing with them. It is true for those of us who are single and fight the battle with extended family members—and a few angels.

What are you praying for God to supply at this time in your walk with Him?

---

1 http://www.imaginis.com/breasthealth/statistics.asp, May 28, 2006 Sources

My Scriptures and Prayer Requests

WHAT ABOUT THE SIDE EFFECTS?

"Not that I speak in regard to need, for I have learned in whatever state I am, to be content: I know how to be abased, and I know how to abound. Everywhere and in all things I have learned both to be full and to be hungry, both to abound and to suffer need. I can do all things through Christ who strengthens me."

- Philippians 4:11-13 (NKJV)

Hair loss happened each time I went through chemo so hats and more hats both times. A gray fedora for hope and a slouch red beanie for an expression of joy plus a slew of other hats donated by friends and coworkers. My hair came back, but a different texture each time. As I've grown older, hair has less significance so going super short was easy.

Be prepared for more new normals as you learn to adjust to a new you from the inside out. In my case, the first time I went through chemo, ordinary scents that I would have ignored, were magnified. Even the ice cubes in my refrigerator seemed to have an unbearable odor. Someone wearing perfumes or colognes created waves of nausea, I'd never experienced before. While I had medications to offset these reactions, they did not completely eliminate them. My nails turned a purplish black. These side effects faded a few months after I completed chemo. Seventeen years later when I went through cancer a second time, the scents and aromas did not bother me, but walking was more difficult and I had to stop frequently. I chose a simple mastectomy without reconstruction but I could not bring myself to look at the surgical site for 2 years. I showered in the dark and avoided mirrors as I could not grapple with my missing body parts. This time as I progressed through chemo, my nails turned dark and fell off though there was no pain. I later learned that the numbness in my fingers and toes were from chemotherapy induced peripheral neuropathy (CIPN) and this condition did not completely go away. My new normals were radically different, but I still thank God for patiently leading me through the challenges. The most important adjustment, above all, was to discuss any and all the changes with my doctors to stay on top of potential problems. As a single person who has learned to push through pain and hardships, it's hard to let go of your independence to ask for help. You learn to share your experiences with your health care professionals and your helpers. You learn to reprioritize and let go of the small things. You let go of pride. Life and living are the most important.

What do you need to release so that you can focus on your coping with side effects?

My Scriptures and Prayer Requests

Life After Treatment...

Being Brave in Other Areas of Your Life

"Therefore strengthen the hands which hang down, and the feeble knees, and make straight paths for your feet, so that what is lame may not be dislocated, but rather be healed."
- Hebrews 12:12-13 (NKJV)

Like other travelers on this cancer journey, being brave does not mean the absence of fear. It means having the faith to move forward anyway. Even the simplest things like shopping for grocery, running the day to day errands and going to work all have challenges. Leaning on God for every step and for the assistance in each trial you face is a must.

Dating

For singles, especially for those who have no children or family nearby, it can be a daunting journey, but God does not leave us alone. Even though I'm now in my 60s, I've still pondered dating as well as participating in my favorite hobby of traveling. God has dealt with me on being self-critical, so I still believe that He may yet have a mate for me. The thought still amuses me as I know God has His own timing on all things.

Job Loss

Both times I struggled with cancer, I lost my job roughly a year after my battle. It would have been easy to be angry, but I see this as God's hand in ending my assignment with that job. Like Moses leaving Egypt for the promised land, when God said move, I moved. (Exodus 12:31-32) Sometimes my move may have been done reluctantly and sometimes as a result of a surprise announcement of a lay-off, but I moved. I've learned that every ending has a new beginning. Like Joshua, I leaned on God's word for being strong and courageous in this journey because He is with me. (Joshua 1:6-9) You can, too.

Like David, I have had to encourage myself in the Lord (1 Samuel 30:6 KJV) as there are no other family members or a spouse to walk with me.

God's grace covers us all during tough times and good times. We seem to notice it more when times are tough. Despite my circumstances, I'll seek God and wait for Him in every area of my life. What about you?

What areas do you need more encouragement and God's comfort?

My Scriptures and Prayer Requests

Your Daily Realities

"Be anxious for nothing, but in everything by prayer and supplication, with thanksgiving, let your requests be made known to God; and the peace of God, which surpasses all understanding, will guard your hearts and minds through Christ Jesus."
- **Philipians 4: 6-7 (NKJV)**

Cancer diagnosis and treatment does not stop the daily realities of life. You may still have a job and have to work. You have bills to pay and treatments to manage. In some ways work actually provides respite and a weird normality to the challenges cancer presents. As a single person, getting rides to and from doctor appointments may be a challenge. Coworkers may try to understand, but no one knows or can experience your reality other than you. Some assume once the treatment is over and you're still alive, that you're cured and everything's fine. Not so. Bosses think you'll be able to work at the same pace with no problem. Wrong. Some people distance themselves from you like cancer is contagious. A myth. Still others who mean well want to treat you like a three-year-old who scraped her knee. Wrong again. Pray for the wisdom and ability to navigate these realities. Each time I've had cancer, I've lost my job not too long after most of the treatments ended. Coincidence? Divine Providence? I don't know, but I trust God with this reality. I see His mercy in these endings. Although the endings made my future a bit precarious, I thank God for the opportunity to adjust to a new normal after cancer.

What daily reality are you praying for God's help?

My Scriptures and prayer requests

Fighting Cancer a Second Time

"And let us not grow weary while doing good, for in due season we shall reap if we do not lose heart."
- Gal 6:9 (NIV)

Cancer is never easy and never wanted, but never quit fighting. That has been my mantra throughout my life and breast cancer has been the biggest challenge I've faced so far. Keep working, keep striving and never stop.

My straw hat reminds me of the work my Mom did as a young woman in rural Mississippi. No job was beneath her. No manual labor too hard. She picked cotton, cleaned other people's homes and kept their children. Any work to support her family was good and she had no complaints on the struggle. My grandmother was the very same way and I witnessed her push through a stroke and still run her business. Both women were warriors in my sight. Though both were long gone before I ever faced cancer, their faith and resilience have been and remain my anchors.

I wear the straw hat for hard work and protection when the heat of the battle is fierce.

Where are you feeling most battle weary? What scriptures will be your anchors?

My Scriptures and Prayer Requests

God's Faithfulness

"And my God shall supply all your need according to His riches in glory by Christ Jesus."
- Philippians 4:19 (NKJV)

"Through the Lord's mercies we are not consumed, because His compassions fail not. They are new every morning; great is Your faithfulness. 'The Lord is my portion,' says my soul, 'Therefore I hope in Him!'"
- Lamentations 3:22-24

The last thing you need is worrying about paying hospital bills when you have a serious disease like cancer. However, treatments are expensive. That's the reality you may be facing. Put on your hat of humility and prayerfully seek help. The battle is to get the right help and there are avenues of support.

Do your research and ask questions. Have friends ask, too. Some insurance plans have navigators who can put you in contact with non-profit agencies that can steer you to financial help. You'll also find there are many services that are free or very low cost like house cleaning, transportation to and from treatments and more. Don't be afraid. Remember, when you are blessed with these services, you are blessing those who provide the blessings. God wastes no suffering, no pain, and no hurt. There is a purpose. Watch His greatness work in your life.

Where do you need God's help in the areas of your financial or care support?

My Scriptures and Prayer Requests

ANSWERING YOUR
Calling

JOURNEY TO RECOVERY

"And we know that all things work together for good to those who love God, to those who are the called according to His purpose."
- Romans 8:28 (NKJV)

God purposefully uses our experiences, whether painful or joyful, for His glory. For those of us experiencing cancer we know this firsthand. The challenge is to open our eyes to what is real and manage the priorities with a sense of urgency. How exactly do we accomplish this?

Here are a few realities I've come to experience on the recovery side of my journey:

- Breast cancer is not a blessing, but there are blessings that God bestows as we walk this journey.
- Being brave and having courage does not mean an absence of fear.
- Experiencing a new normal each time takes time.

When I first was diagnosed….fear, shock, disbelief, anxiety, anger and everything in between rushed through me. I knew of no one in my family who had faced cancer. What caused it? Why must I go through this alone? It took a few days to come to grips with the diagnosis, and I certainly shed a lot of tears.

> *"Therefore humble yourselves under the mighty hand of God, that He may exalt you in due time, casting all your care upon Him, for He cares for you."*
> **- 1 Peter 5:6-7 (NKJV)**

When cancer returned a second time…shock and anger rose in me again, but fear was replaced with a resolute determination to fight. I wasn't truly surprised since I knew cancer could come back even after a 17-year absence. And it did. Cancer returned like an abusive ex showing up on my doorstep. Since I'd been on the journey before, I knew what to expect. Does the previous cancer experience make the journey easier? No.

> *"For You have armed me with strength for the battle; You have subdued under me those who rose up against me."*
> **- Psalm 18:39 (NKJV)**

The first time I experienced cancer, my prayer to God was "please, Lord, I don't want to die." The second time, my prayer was and continues to be "God, I want to live."

The story for me is not over. I live and I thank God every day for life, focused on a future of unknowns, but held by a compassionate Savior. What about you?

> *"Ah, Lord God! Behold, You have made the heavens and the earth by Your great power and outstretched arm. There is nothing too hard for You."*
> **- Jeremiah 32:17 (NKJV)**

Where are you on your journey to recovery?

My Scriptures and prayer requests

www.ingramcontent.com/pod-product-compliance
Lightning Source LLC
LaVergne TN
LVHW010035070426
835507LV00006B/142